THIS
Devotional
belongs to:

_____

_____

GRIEVE, HEAL
& LOVE

31-day Devotional to help you heal while grieving & love yourself through the process.

LAQUELLA BOND

www.TrueVinePublishing.org

Grieve, Heal, Love
LaQuella Bond

Published by True Vine Publishing Co.
810 Dominican Dr.
Nashville, TN 37228
www.TrueVinePublishing.org

ISBN: 978-1-962783-75-0 Paperback
ISBN: 978-1-962783-61-3 eBook

TABLE OF CONTENTS

GRIEVE, HEAL &

Love

LAQUELLA BOND

A 31-DAY DEVOTIONAL

31-day Devotional to help you heal while
grieving & love yourself through the process.

LAQUELLABOND.COM

GRIEVE, HEAL & LOVE

Job lost everything, but God gave him double. May your process--though it may be difficult--be rewarded in Jesus' name. Amen!

GRIEVE, HEAL & LOVE
A 31-Devotional for loss.

This devotional was designed to assist you in healing and loving yourself through the most difficult time of your life while giving you the encouragement to keep going.

INFO@LAQUELLABOND.COM

Social Media
@Laquella Bond

INTRODUCTION

Love is patient, so be patient with yourself. The way you see yourself will determine the outcome of your life. Above all, love each other deeply, because love covers a multitude of sins. (1 Peter 4:8)

Dear friends, let us love one another, for love comes from God. Everyone who loves has been born of God and knows God. (1 John 4:7)

Let all that you do be done in love. (1 Corinthians 16:14)

A new command I give you: Love one another. As I have loved you, so you must love one another. (John 13:34)

And now these three remain: faith, hope, and love. But the greatest of these is love. (1 Corinthians 13:13)

Throughout the Scriptures, God talks about love and how we should hold fast to it. I firmly believe He knew we would need encouragement in this area, so He ensured that love is mentioned 801 times in the NLV Bible.

Hey, there, Love

I AM HERE WITH YOU. DO NOT REPRESS YOUR HEALING!

"GRIEF"
GOD'S, REALITY, INSPIRING, EXEMPLARY, FORTITUDE!

In our grief, we honor those we've lost by holding onto their memories, letting them live within us. Though our loved ones may not be here physically, the impact they've made on our lives remains. Let these memories be a source of comfort and gratitude, and let them remind us to embrace the moments we have today. For one day, these too will be the memories we cherish.

First, I would like to thank God for loving me and entrusting me with the opportunity to write this devotional. I surrender my life to You, God.

I would like to dedicate this book to my wonderful children: Tasia, Amariyon (Lance), my deceased son Malik, who passed away on April 24, 1997, my fantastic mom, who passed away on July 23, 2024, and my sweet granddaughter, Jayla.

I am forever humbled and grateful to each of you who are reading this devotional. My prayer is that it brings light, comfort, and blessings as you navigate your grieving process. May these words support you in finding peace and hope, knowing you're not alone on this journey. May God's love uplift and strengthen you through each step. Grieve, Heal & Love!

"

Healing is a process, & it takes time.

don't rush it

LaQuella Bond

"BELIEVING IN GOD"

DAY 1

Hebrews 11:6 (ESV) - "And without faith, it is impossible to please Him, for whoever would draw near to God must believe that He exists and that He rewards those who seek Him."

My Thoughts

One thing we must do is believe in God wholeheartedly. Believe in the promises of God. BELIEVE GOD IS GOING TO FIX IT AND BRING YOU THROUGH IT. Believe you are the head and not the tail. The devil wants you to doubt God during difficult times. BELIEVE THERE IS ALWAYS HOPE AND VICTORY IN JESUS!

Prayer

Father God, please help my unbelief. ALL THINGS are possible—not some things, but ALL THINGS are possible if I believe. In Jesus' name!

How are you believing God for your situations?

_____

_____

_____

_____

_____

_____

_____

_____

_____

_____

_____

_____

_____

"SERVING GOD "

DAY 2

Scripture

Deuteronomy 10:12 (NIV) - "And now, Israel, what does the Lord your God ask of you but to fear the Lord your God, to walk in obedience to Him, to love Him, to serve the Lord your God with all your heart and with all your soul?"

My Thoughts

Serving means to serve God in all capacities. Remember: God came to serve, not to be served. God, help me to serve. Help me see where I'm called to serve, placing my needs aside to serve and do Your will. Thank You for washing the disciples' feet and showing us the ultimate example of humility and service.

Prayer

Heavenly Father, I love You for showing me how to serve. If everyone would put his or her feelings aside, this world would be a better place. I will serve You through my pain. In Jesus' name, Amen.

How are you serving God in this season of your life?

"SUFFERING WITH GOD"

DAY 3

Scripture
Romans 8:18 (ESV) - "For I consider that the sufferings of this present time are not worth comparing with the glory that is to be revealed to us."

My Thoughts
Don't think God is not watching while you are presently suffering. Keep going—God is going to reveal His glory to you. God sees every tear and hears every prayer. You will never suffer alone; God is with you.

Prayer
Lord, thank You for not leaving me to suffer alone. YOU ARE MY EVERYTHING. In Jesus' name, Amen!

What are you doing during your time of suffering?

_____

_____

_____

_____

_____

_____

_____

_____

_____

_____

_____

"LOVING LIKE GOD"

DAY 4

Scripture

1 Corinthians 13:4-8 (NIV) - "Love is patient, love is kind. It does not envy, it does not boast, it is not proud. It does not dishonor others, it is not self-seeking, it is not easily angered, it keeps no record of wrongs. Love does not delight in evil but rejoices with the truth."

My Thoughts

Love is not a temporary emotional feeling. We should always love the way God loves us. When you are feeling unloved, ask God to wrap His arms around you. God has unconditional love, but people may leave you. God will never stop loving you.

Prayer

God, help me to have unconditional love. I will choose love over hate. Give me a clean heart to love like You. Remove anything that resembles hate. In Jesus' name, Amen!

How are you loving like God?

"BLESSINGS AND FAVOR"

DAY 5

Scripture
Proverbs 11:25 (MSG) - "The one who blesses others is abundantly blessed; those who help others are helped."

My Thoughts
God is leading you to bless others. Let's be truthful—you feel better when you help someone reach their full potential. Try blessing someone when you need a favor from God. God has a blessing with YOUR NAME ON IT!

Prayer
Thank You for blessing me with fruitfulness, long life, prosperity, and perfect health. I praise You, God, in advance for the many blessings and favor to come. I pray this in Your Son Jesus' name, Amen!

How are you blessing others during your time of grief?

"FASTING IN PAIN"

DAY 6

Scripture
Psalm 69:10 (NIV) - "When I weep and fast, I must endure scorn."

My Thoughts
Fasting and praying go hand in hand. Try fasting from food or something you feel like you can't live without. Fasting breaks strongholds, moves mountains, and brings us into the realm of God's power.

Prayer
Father God, please release Your fresh anointing and power to help us go through and reach everything You have for us. Please listen to my heart and sustain me when I feel like giving up. Thank You for Your renewed power. In Jesus' name, Amen!

How are you incorporating fasting and
prayer during this time in your life?

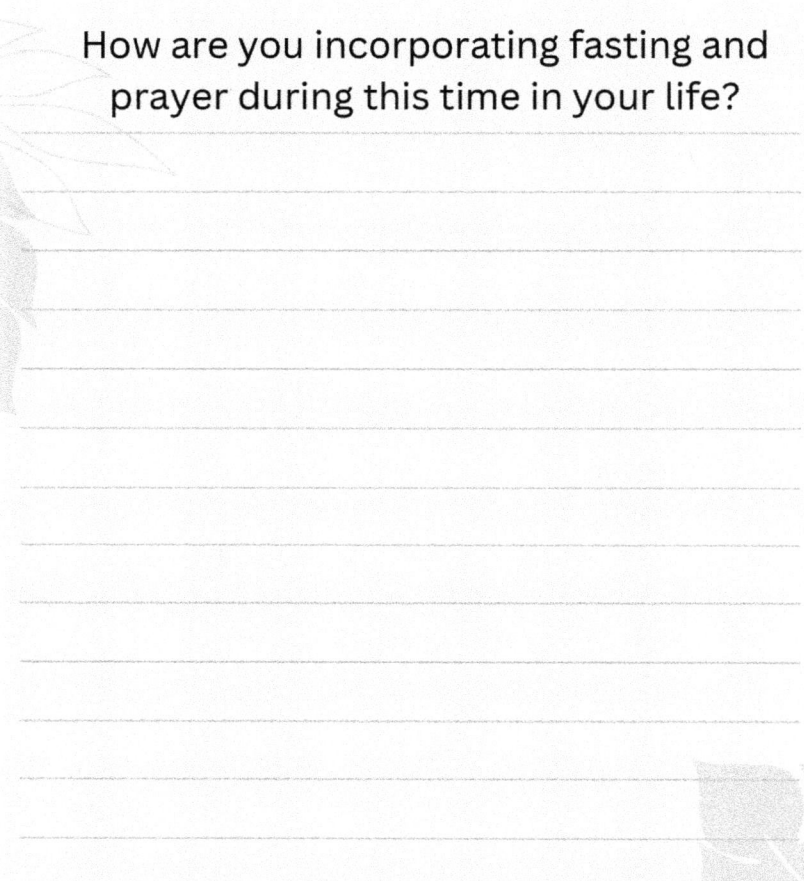

"FORGIVING DURING ADVERSITY"

DAY 7

Scripture

Ephesians 4:32 (NIV) - "Be kind and compassionate to one another, forgiving each other, just as in Christ God forgave you."

My Thoughts

"LET IT GO." Forgive them and give them over to God. If you are having a hard time forgiving, ask God for His help.

Prayer

God, please forgive all my transgressions and release any anger I am holding. Forgiveness is for me, not the other person. Help me to forgive, as You commanded, 7x70 times. In Jesus' name, Amen!

Who do you have to forgive at this time
and how are you doing it?

"HEALING CORRECTLY"

DAY 8

Scripture
Jeremiah 17:4 (KJV) - "Heal me, O Lord and I shall be healed: save me, and I shall be saved: for thou art my praise.

My Thoughts
God is going to heal you everywhere you hurt. Stop accepting partial healing. Ask God to heal you from all diseases and grief that are causing you to be sick. Keep knocking and seeking God until you heal (don't give up). It draws you closer to Him. When you pray, place a demand on your healing. God can't heal what we won't reveal!

Prayer
JEHOVAH RAPHA, (THE GOD THAT HEALS) I'm calling on You for complete healing. Mend my broken heart correctly and replace it with Your love. Help me to release anyone or anything that is a hindrance to my healing. Heal me in Jesus' name, Amen!

Do you feel like you are healing correctly, and if so, how?

"MINISTERING WHILE BLEEDING"

DAY 9

Scripture
1 Peter 4:10-11 (NIV): - "Each of you should use whatever gift you have received to serve others, as faithful stewards of God's grace in its various forms. If anyone speaks, they should do so as one who speaks the very words of God."

My Thoughts
Ministering is doing the Lord's work every day despite how you feel. Whether you are hurting, grieving, sick, sad, or lonely, you must remember that God is still in control! Ask God to pour into you as you minister and pour out to others.

Prayer
God, send Your Spirit to help me minister to Your people. It is not about me and my feelings, but all about You and Your Kingdom. In Jesus' name, Amen!

Are you ministering while bleeding, and if so, how?

"PRAYING WORKS"

DAY 10

Scripture
PHILIPPIANS 4:6 (NIV) - Do not be anxious about anything, but in every situation, by prayer and supplication. (petition) with thanksgiving, present your request to God.

My Thoughts
Pray for God's will, pray for what you need, pray for his wisdom. It doesn't matter where you are-prayer room, car, or work. Pray, because God hears all our prayers. Pray and believe God is going to answer.

Prayer
GOD, help me to believe whatever I ask in prayer, if it is in your will, it shall be granted! In Jesus' mighty name, Amen!

What does your prayer life look like?

"

God is loving you through this...

Trust Him

LaQuella Bond

"GIVING GOD GLORY"

DAY 11

Scripture
ROMANS 15:6 (KJV) - That ye may with one mind and one mouth glorify God, even the father of our Lord Jesus Christ.

My Thoughts
We must be willing to do anything for God's glory, including worshiping, spending time, and sharing the gospel of Jesus Christ. We must do whatever it takes to get what we need from God! I remember giving God the glory with tears in my eyes. I was broken, and I needed to be in His presence.

Prayer
DEAR GOD, help me to give You glory in all things. You are so worthy of all our praise! Glory Hallelujah!

What are you doing to give God the glory
during this time in your life?

"EXPERIENCING GOD"

DAY 12

Scripture
PSALM 34:8 (KJV) - Oh, taste and see that the Lord is good:

My Thoughts
Whenever I was having a bad day, I desperately needed to be in God's presence. Experiencing God is learning to hear his voice and feel His Holy Spirit.

Prayer
Jehovah Nissi, (THE LORD MY BANNER) Thank You so much for always being a present help in times of trouble. You are the banner we need to defeat and protect us from ANY battle. In Jesus' mighty name- Amen!

Do you feel like you are experiencing God on a different level?

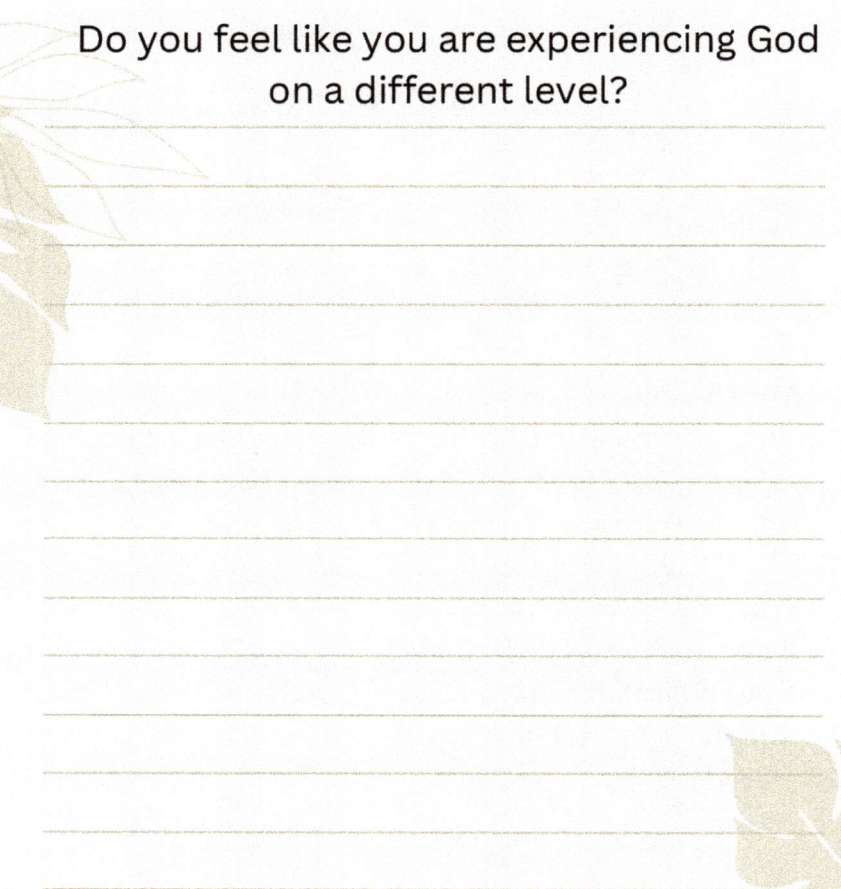

"CRYING WITH SORROW"

DAY 13

Scripture
PSALMS 18:6 (NKJV) - In my distress, I called upon the Lord and cried out to my God: He heard my voice from His temple, and my cry came before Him, even to His ears.

My Thoughts
Crying is not a sign of weakness; it is a sign of meekness and strength. Let go and let God! God is holding you when you cry. I'm a witness, God will leave the 99 and come see about the one. John 11:35 Jesus wept" It reveals aspects of His human nature.

Prayer
HEAVENLY FATHER, Thank You for coming to see about me when I was in distress. Your gentleness comforted me through my tears. Hallelujah in Jesus' name, Amen!

How are you giving your sorrow to God?

"STANDING STILL"

DAY 14

Scripture
PSALM 46:10 (NIV) - Be still and know that I am God:
I will be exalted among the nations, I will be exalted in
the earth.

My Thoughts
When God says to be still He is trying to reveal His
plans to you. In other words -relax, chill, and wait on
Him. We will often try to make wrong moves and quick
decisions without God. Learn to stand still, and God will
move on our behalf.

Prayer
JEHOVAH-ROHI, (GOD OUR SHEPHERD) I will
trust You, be patient, stop striving, and wait on You. I
will stand still and see Your salvation in Jesus' name
Amen!

Are you standing still and allowing God
to care for you?

"WORSHIP & PRAISE"

DAY 15

Scripture
PSALM 100:1 (NIV) - Worship the Lord with gladness: come before Him with joyful songs.

My Thoughts
Whenever you are feeling overwhelmed by grief, try your best to worship God with praise, singing and giving. Praising God always ushers in His spirit. Praise allows God to listen to your heart. When we worship SOMETHING has to BREAK!!

Prayer
JEHOVAH MEKADESH (GOD WHO SANCTIFIES)
Listen to my heart as I worship You in spirit and truth. You are never far away when we worship. In Jesus' name, Amen!

What are you doing to worship God and
give Him the glory?

"REPRESENTING GOD"

DAY 16

Scripture

2 CORINTHIANS 5:20 (NKJV) - Now then we are ambassadors for Christ, as though God were pleading through us: we implore you on Christ's behalf be reconciled to God.

My Thoughts

While going through the storms of life, we should always be a representative of Jesus, It shows others how to go through. You never know who is watching you to see how you represent God.

Prayer

HEAVENLY FATHER, I know that integrity is important to You, and as Christians, we should always represent You no matter who is watching. God, help me to be a great representative of your word. In Jesus' name, Amen!

How are you representing God during this challenging time?

"STAYING CONNECTED TO GOD"

DAY 17

Scripture

JOHN 15: 5-6 (NKJV) - I am the vine, you are the branches. He who abides in me, and I in him, bears much fruit: for without me you can do nothing. If anyone does not abide in me, he is cast out as a branch and is withered; and they gather them and throw them into the fire.

My Thoughts

I would often have thoughts to disconnect from God, because of my pain. But, just like a tree, if a branch falls off it will die. We must always stay connected to God. Everything connected to God grows.

Prayer

FATHER GOD, help me to always stay connected to You, I know if I disconnect from You, it will result in my spirit dying. I will not let You go until You bless me. In Jesus' mighty name, Amen!

What are you doing to stay connected to God?

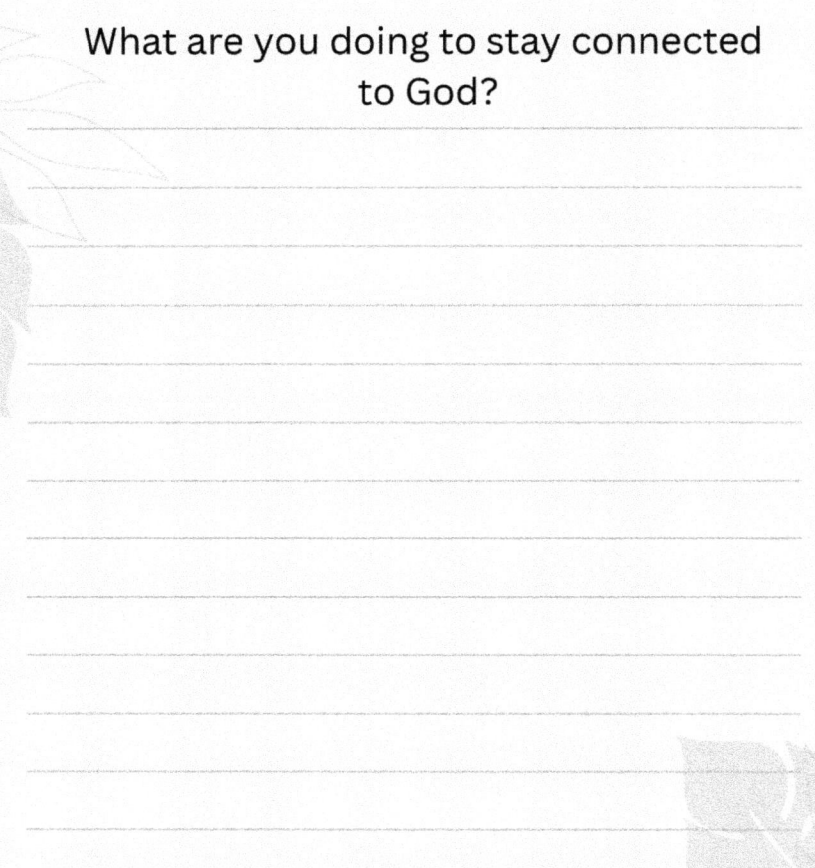

"INTIMACY WITH GOD"

DAY 18

Scripture
John 10:27 (NIV) - My sheep listen to my voice: I know them, and they follow me.

My Thoughts
"Is that You speaking, God"? If we are praying to hear His voice, He is speaking to us. We must be willing to listen and be intimate with God about everything, even the difficult circumstances we are dealing with. Sometimes you must turn off the distractions to be intimate with God.

Prayer
GOD, You are amazing! Teach us how to become more intimate with You. Continue to give us ears to hear to discern Your voice, so we can be obedient to Your promises. Help us to honor You forever in Jesus' name, Amen!

Are you being intentional in being intimate with God?

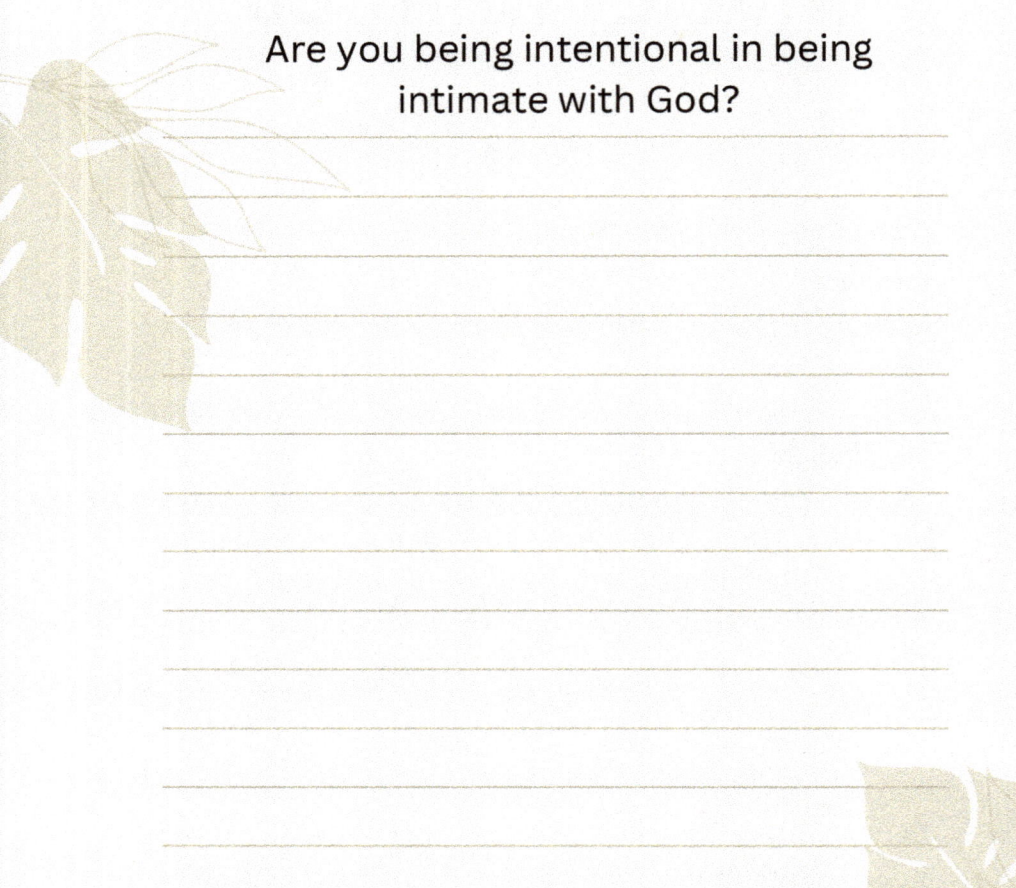

"EMPOWERED BY THE HOLY SPIRIT"

DAY 19

Scripture
JOHN 15:26 (NIV) - Jesus promised to send the Holy Spirit to empower and guide his followers.

My Thoughts
Listen to the Holy Spirit when you feel weak and reach out to Him. God is always there and is willing to pull you out of the dark places.

Prayer
JEHOVAH, Help me to stay empowered with Your word, no matter the situation. I need Your anointed power daily. I'm asking these things in Your Son Jesus' name, Amen!

Are you allowing yourself to be empowered by the Holy Spirit?

"RECEIVING WHILE GRIEVING"

DAY 20

Scripture

MARK 11:24 (NKJV) - Therefore, I say to you, whatever things you ask when you pray, believe that you receive them, and you will have them.

My Thoughts

God, I am petitioning You for peace, healing, and love. I believe in my spirit that you will give me the desires of my heart as long as it is in Your perfect will for my life.

Prayer

HEAVENLY, FATHER, I know You will provide for my every need according to Your riches in glory. Thank you, in advance for answering my prayer! It's already done in the mighty name, of Jesus. Amen!

Explain how you are allowing yourself to receive blessings in your life right now.

"

your testimony is
helping others...
don't quit

LaQuella Bond

"THANKFUL FOR YOU GOD"

DAY 21

Scripture

1 THESSALONIANS 5:18 (NIV) - Be thankful in all circumstances, for this is God's will for you, who belong to Christ Jesus.

My Thoughts

Give thanks in everything, storms, death, rejection. God help us to have a thankful heart! God has his hands on you. Always thank God for what is to come, favor, peace, protection, and redirection. God is going to provide. You will win!

Prayer

FATHER GOD, thank You so much for sending Jesus to die for our sins. I am forever thankful for what I have and what is to come.! Thank You, for Your mercy, and grace because I fall short every day. In Jesus' name, Amen!

How are you showing God that you're thankful for Him in your situation?

"GROWING & FLOURISHING SPIRITUALLY"

DAY 22

Scripture
PSALM 92: 12-13 (NIV) - The righteous will flourish like a palm tree, they will grow like a cedar of Lebanon: planted in the house of the Lord, they will flourish in the courts of God.

My Thoughts
I know without a shadow of doubt that my relationship with God flourished while I was grieving. Always pray for spiritual growth, We should not be the same person if we have made the conscious decision to grow every day. Flourish wherever you are planted!

Prayer
Dear God, command me to flourish and grow in Your word. I am asking You to change everything that is not like You. I thank You for the fruits of the spirit! In Jesus' name, Amen!

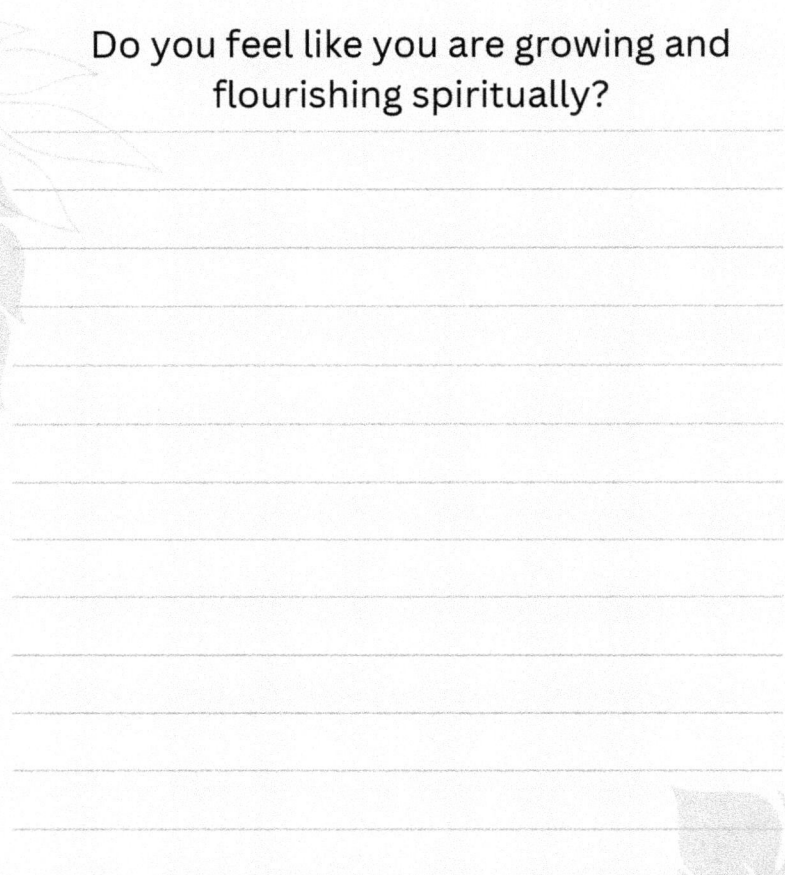

Do you feel like you are growing and
flourishing spiritually?

"RESTORATION AFTER SUFFERING"

DAY 23

Scripture
1 PETER: 5:10 (ESV) - And after you have suffered a little while, the God of all grace, who has called you to his eternal glory in Christ, will himself restore, confirm, strengthen and establish you.

My Thoughts
Restore whatever is broken in my life. Make things better in my heart, my mind, and my relationships. I have been suffering for a while. I need You, not tomorrow, but right now, Lord.

Prayer
GOD, please forgive my sins and restore me. I'm broken God, only You can restore me. Fix me, Lord, in Your Son Jesus' name, Amen!

Do you believe that you will experience restoration after your suffering?

"CONFIRMATION & COURAGE"

DAY 24

Scripture
Joshua 1:9 (NIV) - "Be strong and courageous: do not be dismayed, for the Lord your God is with you wherever you go."

My Thoughts
God will often confirm who He is by using signs, evidence, and wisdom from others. We must be willing to listen for confirmation from God. Sometimes, God will confirm some things we don't want to hear- don't second guess it, if you asked for confirmation, be encouraged, He is working. Whew, don't ignore your intuition, God gave you that inner voice for a reason.

Prayer
Almighty God, thank You for confirming so many things in our lives. Continue to give us 'courage and confirmation 'to accept Your will. In Jesus' name, Amen!

Are you seeing to the confirmation and courage that God is providing?

_____

_____

_____

_____

_____

_____

_____

_____

_____

_____

_____

"LIVING LIFE ABUNDANTLY"

DAY 25

Scripture
John 10:10 (AMP) - The thief comes only to steal and kill and destroy, I came that they may have and enjoy life, and have it in abundance (to the full, till it overflows).

My Thoughts
SEEK FIRST THE KINGDOM OF GOD. We should always be content, no matter what life throws at us. Live as a child of God, and die to our flesh daily. Is It Easy? No, not always, but If we want our lives to be abundantly blessed, we must obey.

Prayer
Lord, I'm going to live my life for you, I want to experience the fullness of joy and strength in my spirit, soul, and body all the days of my life. What You give, no man can take it away. In Jesus' name, Amen!

Are you positioning yourself to live life abundantly in spite of?

"SACRIFICING MY LIFE FOR YOU"

Scripture
Romans 12:1 (ESV) - I appeal to you therefore, brothers, by the mercies of God, to present your bodies as a living sacrifice, holy and acceptable to God which is your spiritual worship.

My Thoughts
Wow! God made the ultimate sacrifice for us. How can we not sacrifice our time, treasure, talent, etc., to live for Him? God, help us to be at your mercy to reap all the benefits of the Kingdom.

Prayer
Father God, lead me to be a living sacrifice. Use me, Lord, I want to forever live according to the purpose You have for my life. You have all the power and authority to move me out of your way. I pray these things in Your Son Jesus' name, Amen!

How are you sacrificing your life for God?

_____
_____
_____
_____
_____
_____
_____
_____
_____
_____
_____
_____

"FAITHFULLY TRUSTING GOD"

DAY 27

Scripture

Proverbs 3:3-5 (ESV) - Let not steadfast love and faithfulness forsake you; bind them around your neck; write them on the tablet of your heart. So, you will find favor and success in the sight of God and man. Trust in the Lord with all your heart, and DO NOT lean on your understanding.

My Thoughts

Being faithful means being loyal and following His commandments. Being faithful and trusting God is believing His word. We are to fully rely on GOD even when we want to choose our path. We are to be faithful to everything God has entrusted us with. I trust You, Lord.

Prayer

God, I know You allow HURTFUL situations to happen in our lives to see if we will continue to trust and be faithful to You. My answer is Yes! I will be FAITHFUL because I know You are holding me through all my heartache. In Jesus' name, I will continue to be faithful to You. Amen!

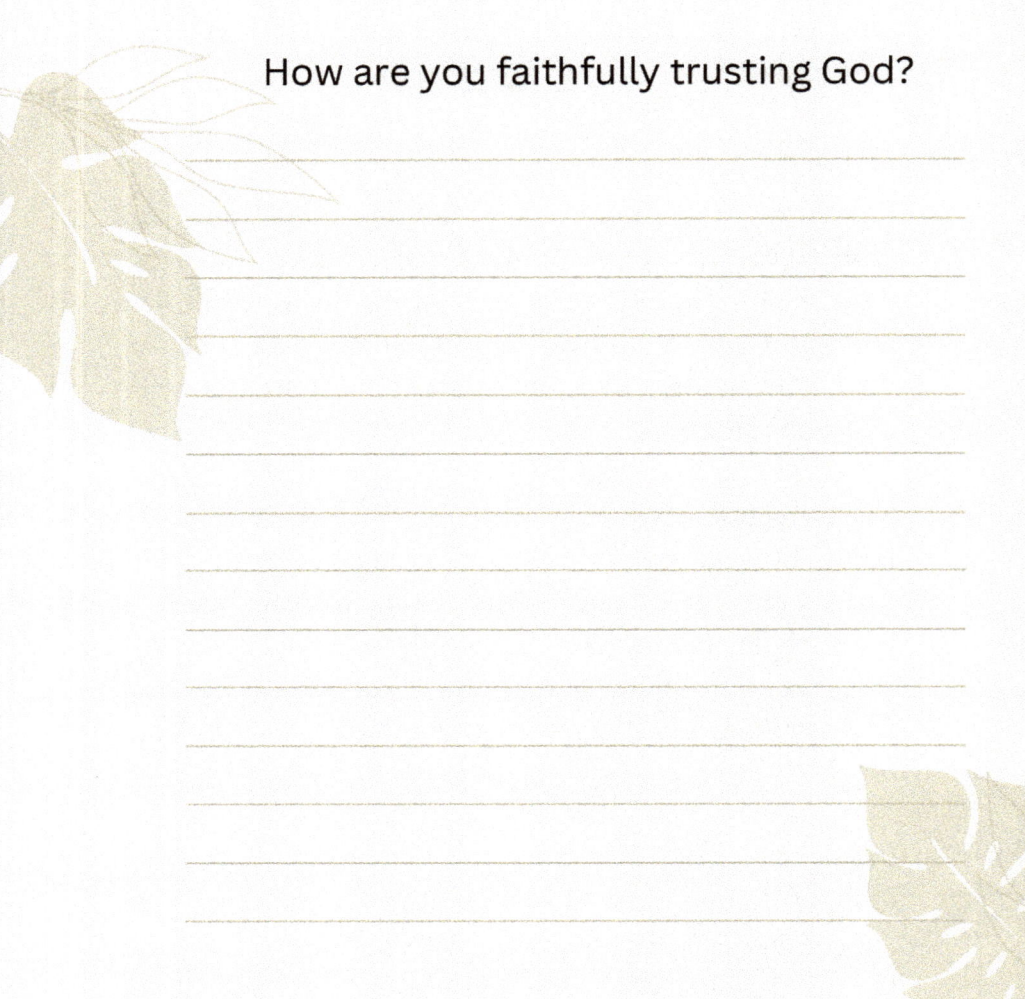

How are you faithfully trusting God?

"PERFECT PEACE OR SHALOM"

DAY 28

Scripture

JOHN 14:27 (NIV) - Peace, I leave with you; I give you peace. Not as the world gives; do I give to you. Let not your hearts be troubled, neither let them be afraid.

My Thoughts

I need You to guard my heart and mind against anxiety, and stress. I will believe in Your promises for perfect peace. Remove discontentment, unhappiness, and strife that is causing me a lack of peace. I will always take your peace (SHALOM) for my weakness.

Prayer

PRINCE OF PEACE, I come to You today commanding Your perfect peace and expecting You to sustain me. I will not let my heart be troubled. I need Your outward and inward peace to live day by day. You said whatever we ask in Your son, Jesus' name will be granted. God, I request this and more for me daily. Peace be still in the name of JESUS!

Are you allowing yourself to release
anxiety and rest in perfect peace?

"SURVIVING THE STORMS"

DAY 29

Scripture
2 Corinthians 4:8-9 (NIV) - We are hard pressed on every side, but not crushed; perplexed, but not in despair; persecuted, but not destroyed.

My Thoughts
I remember being in survival mode. I was hopeless, unmotivated, and defeated. I had to remind myself, that I was traumatized by my son's untimely death which gave me a reason to feel lost. I heard God say, "It won't always be like this" WEEPING MAY ENDURE FOR A NIGHT, BUT JOY COMES IN THE MORNING!

Prayer
Lord, help us to realize, that You didn't place us here on earth just to live in survival mode, but You called us here to thrive and be MORE THAN CONQUERORS. Thank You, Lord, for being my firm foundation. In Jesus' name, Amen!

Are you trusting God to survive your storm?

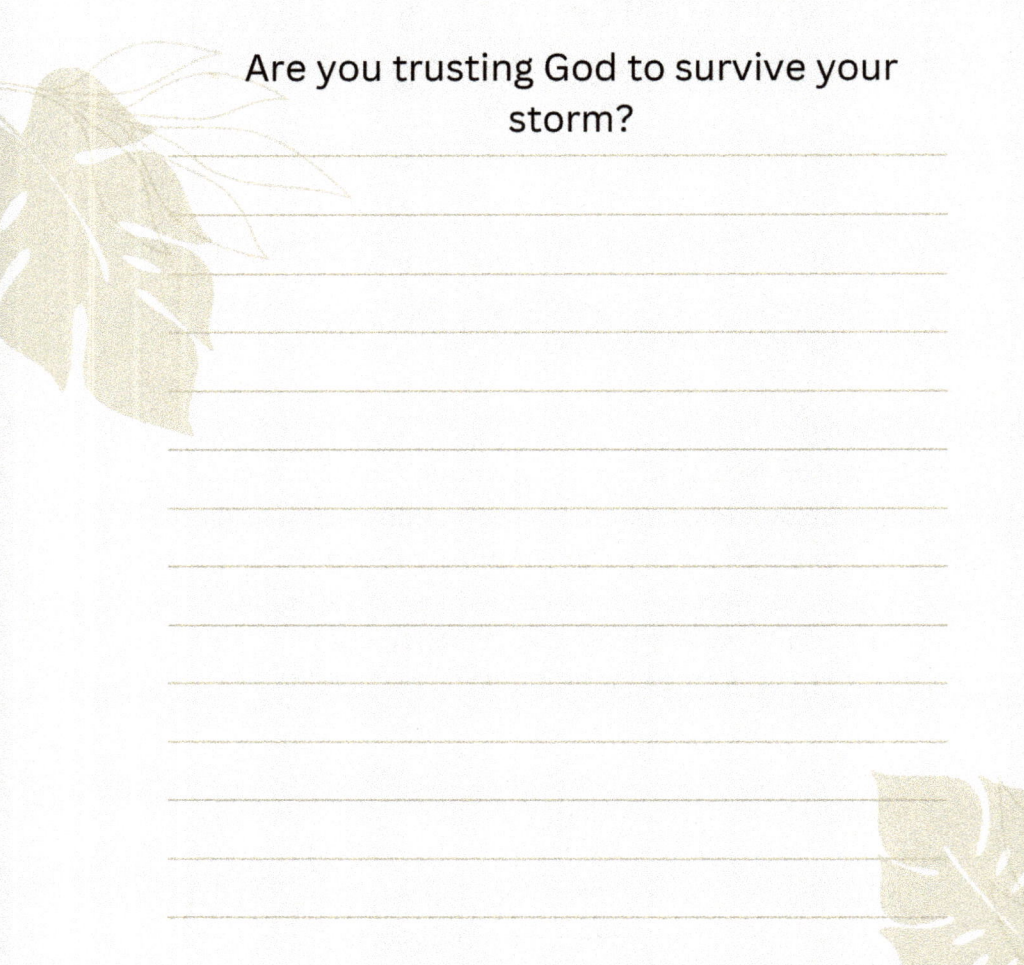

"OPPOSITION TO VICTORY"

Day 30

Scripture

1 John 5:4-5 (ESV) - For everyone who has been born of God overcomes the world. And this is the victory that has overcome the world of our faith. Who is it that overcomes the world except the one who believes that Jesus is the son of God?

My Thoughts

God wants us to know that we **already** have the victory over our opposition and fears. We will **defeat** the enemy!! If God be for us, who can be against us? Defeat can't stay where Victory is! We will win if we don't give up. Victory belongs to Jesus!

Prayer

Father God, help me to endure adversity when it comes. You are my Shepherd, I shall not fear, I have victory over all things that come my way. I am fearfully and wonderfully made. I know You are strengthening me for all the battles here on earth. In Jesus' name, Amen!

What are you doing to fight the opposition
that's trying to steal your victory?

_____

_____

_____

_____

_____

_____

_____

_____

_____

_____

_____

_____

"THE DAY OF SALVATION"

Day 31

Scripture
Romans 10: 9-10 (NIV) - That if you confess with your mouth, "Jesus is Lord," and believe in your heart that God raised him from the dead, you will be saved. For it is with your heart that you believe and are justified, and it is with your mouth that you confess and are saved."

My Thoughts
I am so glad that God doesn't require much for us to be saved. He asks that we believe, confess, and accept him into our hearts. The day I was saved and invited God into my heart was the best day of my life. I never did look back. I know I am on the right journey for my life.

Prayer
Dear Lord, Thank you for dying on the cross for sinners like us. We love and praise you, FOREVER! In Jesus' name!

Have you accepted the Lord Jesus Christ
as your savior? If not, why?

_____

_____

_____

_____

_____

_____

_____

_____

_____

_____

_____

"SINNING AND BLASPHEMY"

Scripture
JOHN 1:10 (NIV) - If we claim we have not sinned, we make God out to be a liar and his word is not in us.

My Thoughts
Often, when we ARE GRIEVING, we WILL experience a void, that we will TRY to replace by sinning. Guess what? Only, God can fill that void.

OFTENTIMES, the devil will persuade us to sin, that is when we need to pray MORE. Yes, we can repent, but sin can and will become an ungodly habit to break. JESUS PAID THE ULTIMATE PRICE FOR OUR SINS.

Prayer
Yahweh, I come pleading and asking You to help us to sin-less even though we are human and will fall short. God, You are the only perfect one. God, help us to pray whenever we are tempted to sin. Yahweh, help us not to listen to the devil, he is from the pits of hell. Satan, you must flee from us. God, I love You more than anything! Amen, Amen!

Have you repented of your sins?

"Cherishing the Moments"

We often don't recognize the best times of our lives until they become cherished memories we hold close, especially when they involve loved ones who are no longer with us. Those simple moments — the laughter, shared meals, and even the quiet times — gain new meaning.

Sitting here with tears flowing — yes, I said tears — it is perfectly okay to cry. Cry as much and as often as you need to. God will heal you and hold you the entire time you are crying. You are His child. God loves you more than you will ever know.

Trust God with everything in you until you feel His holy presence. Don't give up! Tell God you can't heal correctly without Him. God will always be with you the entire time you are grieving. God will heal your broken heart! He is so close to the brokenhearted. Always put on the "Full Armor of God":
- The belt of truth
- The breastplate of righteousness
- The gospel of peace
- The shield of faith
- The helmet of salvation
- The sword of the Spirit

Thank You, Father God, for giving me the strength to humbly write this devotional for everyone who is grieving. God, I know You made the ultimate sacrifice when You gave Your Son, Jesus, to die for our sins. I will forever be grateful. Thank You for trusting me to raise Malik for three years.

HALLELUJAH!! There is none like You Father!

GRIEVING is such a personal journey, and leaning into God's presence can offer immense comfort and strength. Holding onto His unchanging hands can remind you that no matter how turbulent life feels, He remains constant and compassionate.

Sometimes, our expectations of others can lead to disappointment, especially during challenging times like grief. People care but have their struggles and commitments. By having a steady relationship with God, we gain a source of support that never wavers, even when others may not be available.

When we all get to heaven, we all want to hear God say "Well done thy good and faithful servant."

About the Author

LaQuella Bond

My name is LaQuella Bond, I am a compassionate writer, coach, and speaker who understands the deep pain of loss and the powerful process of healing. Having walked my own path of grief, I created Grieve, Heal & Love to offer others the comfort and encouragement I found in my journey. Through my personal experiences and spiritual insights, I hope to guide others toward peace, healing, and rediscovering love.

I was born in Jackson, TN moved to Paducah, KY where my journey began. I have been married twice and divorced twice. I have two wonderful living children Tasia, Amariyon, and one (deceased) son Malik, and a beautiful granddaughter Jayla.

I wouldn't change my journey for anything.

laquellabond.com

Notes

Notes

Notes

Notes

**A Thank You Letter
From LaQuella**

Dear Friend,

Thank you for taking the time to invest in
yourself by reading this devotional. It is
my hope that you have received everything
you were desiring.

Your quality of life is important to me. I
pray that you find yourself in a place of
surrender and healing. You are wonderfully
created in the image of God.

I look forward to your growth. If you need
help navigating life, Connect with me.

With Love

Laquella

**Your Sister In Christ
LAQUELLA BOND**

Grieve , Heal & Love

Grieve, Heal & Love is for the person who is dealing with a loss and needs support to navigate the pain. This devotional along with seeking God is a go-to when you need to feel heard and loved.

LaQuella Bond
Author & Loss Advocate

LAQUELLABOND.COM

www.ingramcontent.com/pod-product-compliance
Lightning Source LLC
Chambersburg PA
CBHW051230120626
46547CB00013B/1588